A Note from David Macaulay

Dear reader,

I have been using my eyes for as long as I can remember. Until I got older and needed glasses to read and draw, I never thought much about them. Even though they need a little help these days, they still send lots of great information to my brain. Take care of your eyes and they will do the same for you.

When I was a kid I did not like to read. But if a book had pictures, I would try to read it. The pictures made reading more fun. They helped me understand what the words meant. Words and pictures are still my favorite way to read a story. They are also my favorite way to tell a story. So this book tells you about your eyes in words and shows you in pictures.

David

Dear parents and teachers,

Readers, like the one you are holding, have long served as the portal through which children can be lured into the world of words. The most successful of these use illustration to soften the hard work of learning to decode text. But children are not only learning verbal literacy, they are learning visual literacy as well. They learn to read pictures, to pick up clues that may help them infer meaning and add depth to the words.

All the topics chosen for the books in this series are nonfiction. Whether they are historical or contemporary, from the natural world or the manmade, the topics reflect things we know children are interested in and curious about. Since these books are intended to stimulate both verbal and visual literacy, each page is balanced and information is conveyed in both art and text.

To support the reader's curiosity, there is a glossary, list of suggested books and other media, and an index in the back of the book.

It is my hope that these books will connect future citizens with their increasingly complex planet in a meaningful and creative way. If I've done my job well, you will enjoy reading and looking, too.

David Macaulay

For activities and reading tips, visit myreadersonline.com.

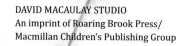

DAVID MACAULAY STUDIO
An imprint of Roaring Brook Press/
Macmillan Children's Publishing Group

Printed in China by Toppan Leefung Printing Ltd., Dongguan City,
Guangdong Province
For information, address Macmillan Children's Publishing Group,
175 Fifth Avenue, New York, NY 10010.

Library of Congress Control Number: 2012951526

ISBN 978-1-59643-781-4 (hardcover)
10 9 8 7 6 5 4 3 2 1
ISBN 978-1-59643-782-1 (paperback)
10 9 8 7 6 5 4 3 2 1

First Edition: 2013

mackids.com

This is a Level 4 book
LEXILE AD640L

DAVID MACAULAY

EYE
How It Works

with

SHEILA KEENAN

Stick with me, kids!

Aye, aye, sir.

David Macaulay Studio
Macmillan Children's Publishing Group
New York

It's game day.
One last look.
Cleats? *Check.*

Shin guards in? *Check.*
Socks up? *Check.*

Shorts and shirt?
Whoops!
Better turn that shirt
right side out.
At last you're off to the field.

Most of your team is already there.
Theresa tying her shoes. *Check.*
Alvin chewing his mouth guard. *Check.*
Emma putting up her hair. *Check.*
Roger. *Roger?*
Where is Roger?
Hey! Watch out! There is a soccer ball
coming your way.

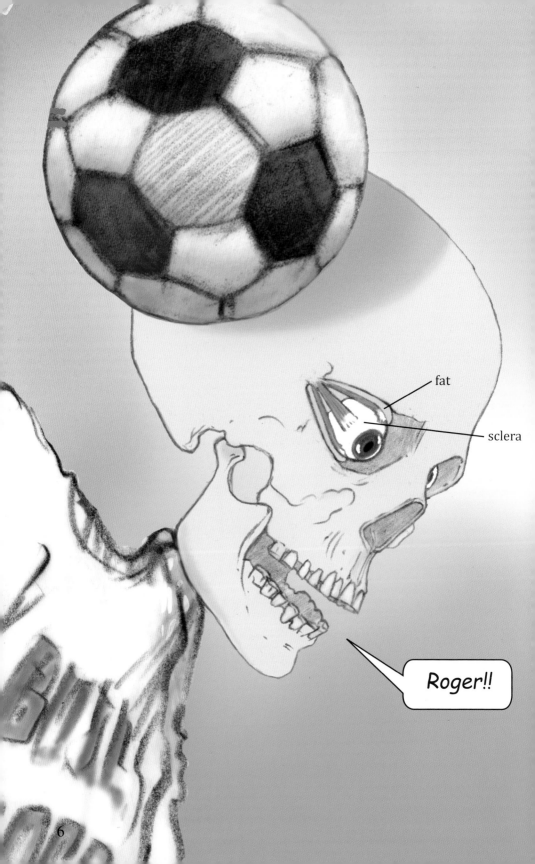

BAM!
It is a good thing each eye is protected
by its own socket in your bony skull.
And each is surrounded by a layer of fat
so it doesn't bang against the bone.

Both eyes also have a strong covering
called the sclera.

Six muscles keep your eyeballs
from popping out.
They also move your eyes
up and down and right and left
so you can see what's going on
around you.

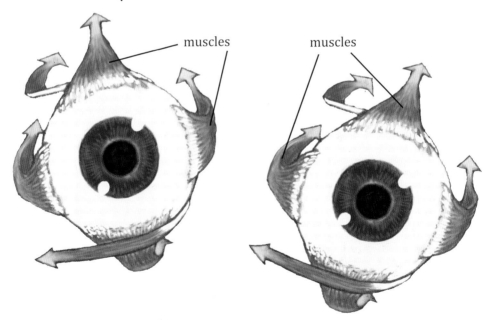

muscles   muscles

Wait a minute!
How did you know
that your shirt was inside out?
How did you know
that Roger was missing?
How did you know
which was your team?

It all starts with light.

Light bounces off everything.
When you look at Roger,
some of the light bouncing off him
goes into your eyes.
Your eyes send this information
to your brain.
It is your brain that tells you
who or what you are
looking at.

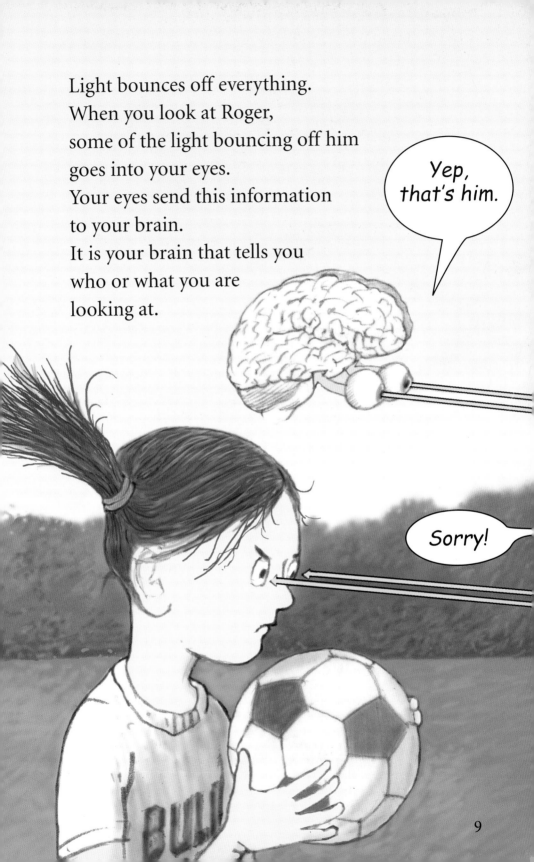

9

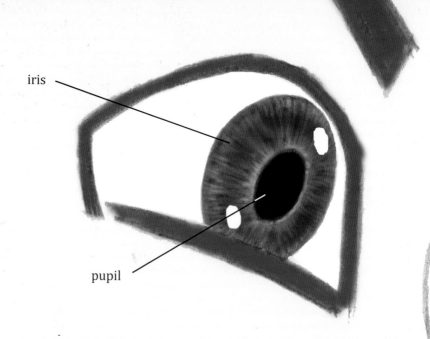

iris

pupil

Light enters each eye through the cornea.
The cornea is the clear surface
at the front of the eye.
When you look in the mirror
the cornea looks shiny.
The curve of the cornea bends the light
toward a dark, round opening in the eyeball.
That opening is called the pupil.
The pupil is at the center of the iris,
which can be brown, gray, green, blue
or even speckled!

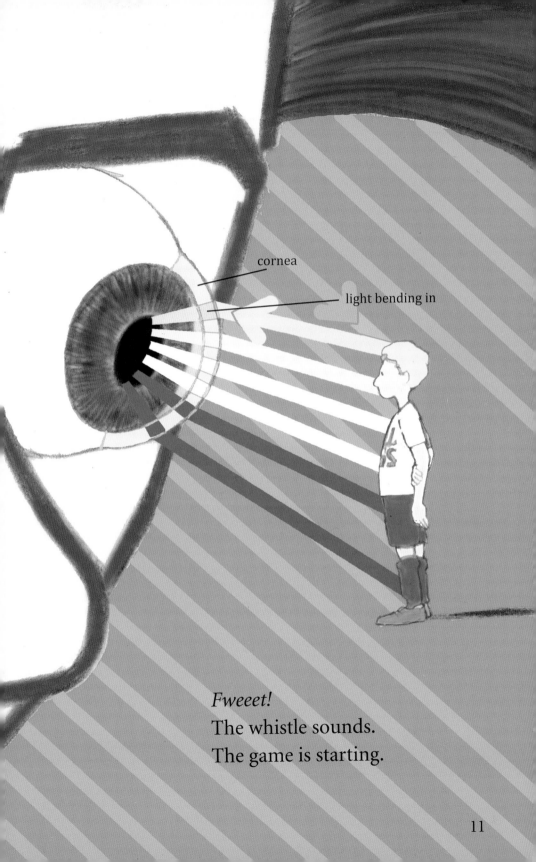

cornea

light bending in

Fweeet!
The whistle sounds.
The game is starting.

The iris controls the size of the pupil.
Today, the bright sun is shining.
Your iris closes down the pupil
to let in just the right amount of light.
If it were cloudy, your iris would open up
the pupil to capture more light.
You feel yourself squinting.
That shuts out some light, too.
Too much strong sunlight
will damage your eyes.

No problem seeing the ball today though.
As long as you're looking
in the right direction.
BAM!

Roger!

Sorry!

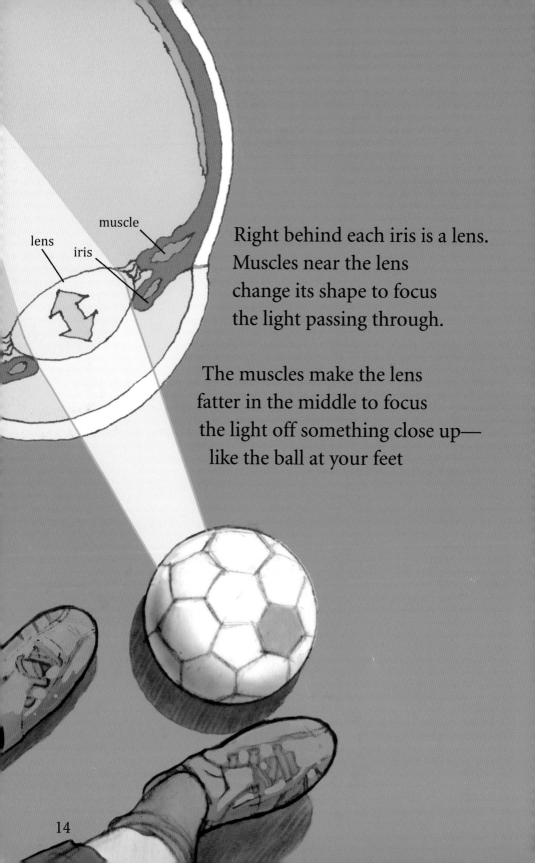

muscle

lens

iris

Right behind each iris is a lens.
Muscles near the lens
change its shape to focus
the light passing through.

The muscles make the lens
fatter in the middle to focus
the light off something close up—
like the ball at your feet

They make the lens thinner
to focus the light from
things that are farther away.
The lens keeps changing shape
as those far away things get closer.

15

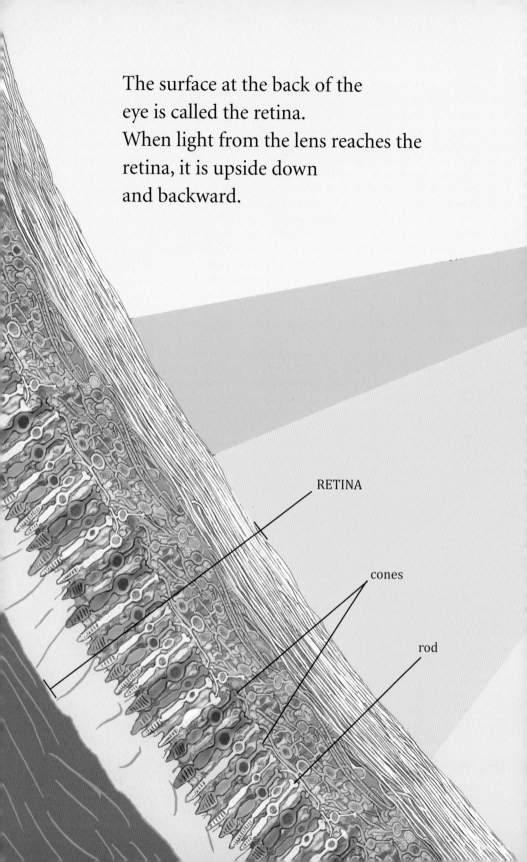

The surface at the back of the
eye is called the retina.
When light from the lens reaches the
retina, it is upside down
and backward.

RETINA

cones

rod

This light carries information about
shape, color, size, distance, and motion.
But your brain can't work with light.

Cells in the retina called rods and cones
change the light information into signals
that the brain can understand.
Rods send information about
how light or dark an object is.
Cones send information about colors.
There are about 100 million rods
 and 7 million cones in each eye
so you don't miss a thing!

There goes the whistle for half time.
Let's go over the game so far.

Light enters each eye
through the cornea.

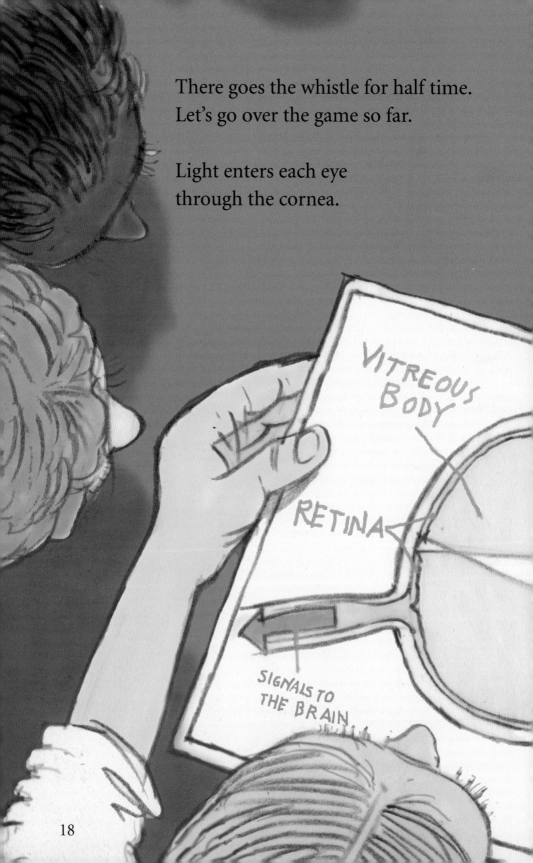

VITREOUS BODY

RETINA

SIGNALS TO THE BRAIN

It passes through the pupil in the iris
and then through the lens.
The lens focuses the light on the retina
at the back of the eye.
On the way to the retina,
light passes through the vitreous body.
This jelly-like mass helps give the eye its shape.
Rods and cones send signals from the eye
to the brain.

Fweeeet!
The second half is
starting.
Go Bull Dogs!

Signals from the retina travel
along nerve fibers to the brain.
These fibers come together to make
thick cables called optic nerves.
One optic nerve comes from
the back of each eye.

optic nerve

LEFT EYE

You have two eyes for two reasons. First, for backup just in case something happens to one of your eyes. Second, so you can see things in 3-D. This helps you avoid charging Tigers and high-speed soccer balls.

signals to the brain

RIGHT EYE

TIGERS

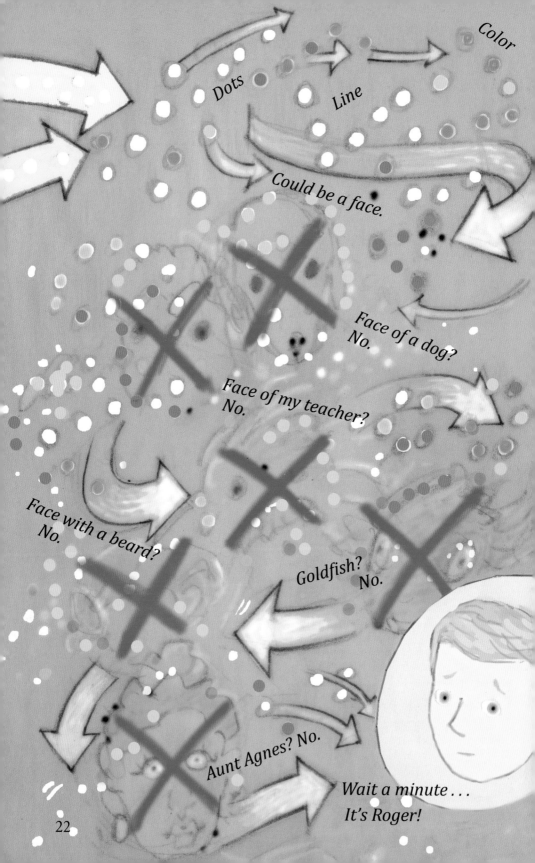

Your brain remembers most of the things
you have seen in your life.
As the signals rush in,
brain cells look for a match
between the new information
and everything you've seen before.
That's how you recognized Roger!

You look at the scoreboard.
Your brain tells you
the game is almost over.
You had better get moving!

Suddenly, you fall flat on your face.
There goes Sarah!
Even with her flashy new sports specs
she ran right into you.

Not all eyeballs are perfectly shaped.
Sometimes the light that hits the retina
is not focused.
Glasses, contact lenses, and flashy
sports specs have lenses that bend light
so it hits the retina just right.

Usually.

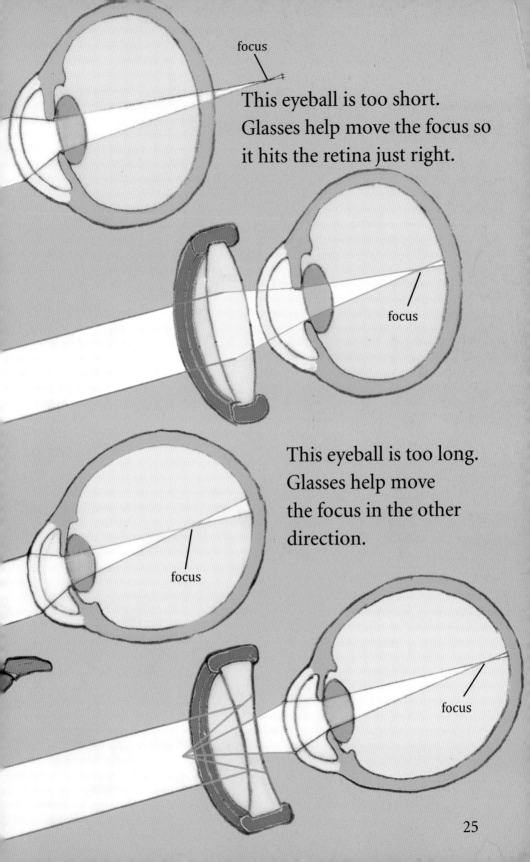

focus

This eyeball is too short.
Glasses help move the focus so
it hits the retina just right.

focus

This eyeball is too long.
Glasses help move
the focus in the other
direction.

focus

focus

25

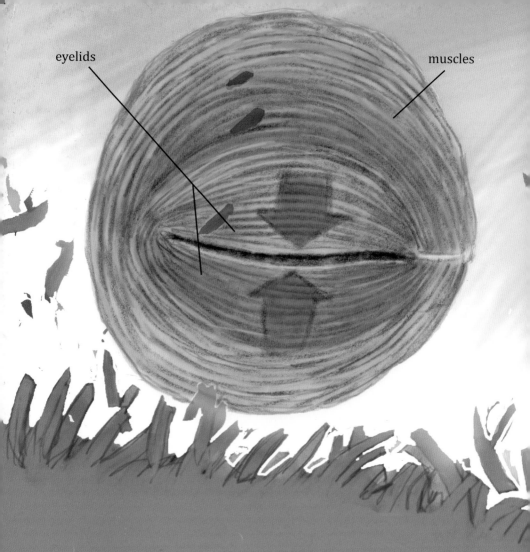

eyelids

muscles

It feels like you have half the field
on your face.

Because your eyes are so important to you
they are very well cared for.
As soon as you hit the ground
muscles closed your eyes.
Tears started to flow
from a gland above each eye.

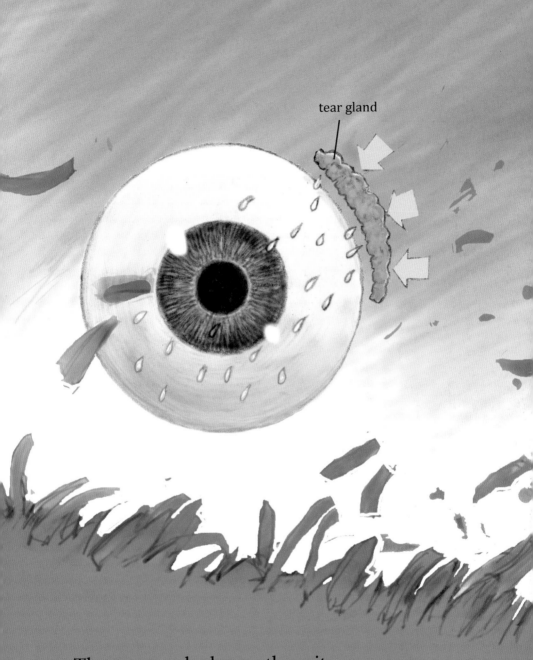

tear gland

The tears washed away the grit.
Every time you blink, tears coat your eyes.
This keeps them clean and moist.
Eyelashes stop most germs, dust, and
flying sand from getting in.

Only five seconds left
and you never once had to tell
your eyes what to do.
You just had to keep them open.
Your eyes and your brain are a great team.

And speaking of teams,
out of the corner of your eye you see Roger.
He has kicked the ball right at you.
Again.
But this time, you are ready.
Bam.
You head the ball right into the net.
You've won the game!

WORDS TO KNOW

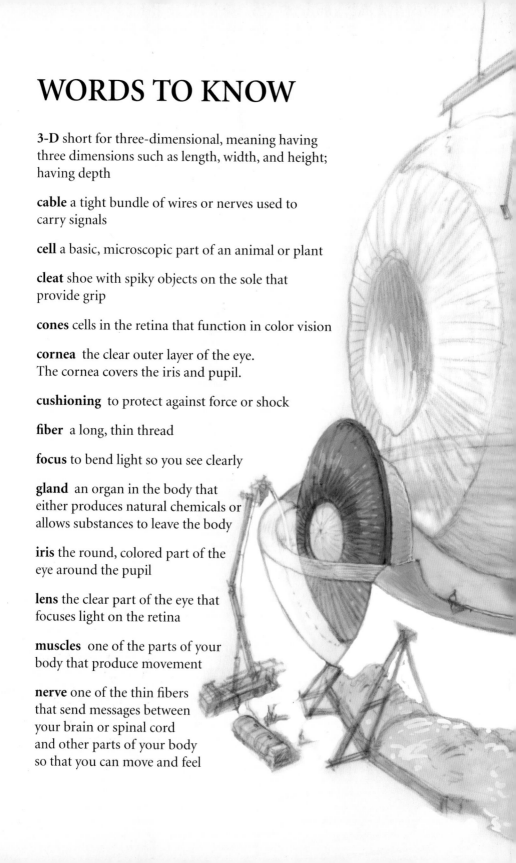

3-D short for three-dimensional, meaning having three dimensions such as length, width, and height; having depth

cable a tight bundle of wires or nerves used to carry signals

cell a basic, microscopic part of an animal or plant

cleat shoe with spiky objects on the sole that provide grip

cones cells in the retina that function in color vision

cornea the clear outer layer of the eye. The cornea covers the iris and pupil.

cushioning to protect against force or shock

fiber a long, thin thread

focus to bend light so you see clearly

gland an organ in the body that either produces natural chemicals or allows substances to leave the body

iris the round, colored part of the eye around the pupil

lens the clear part of the eye that focuses light on the retina

muscles one of the parts of your body that produce movement

nerve one of the thin fibers that send messages between your brain or spinal cord and other parts of your body so that you can move and feel

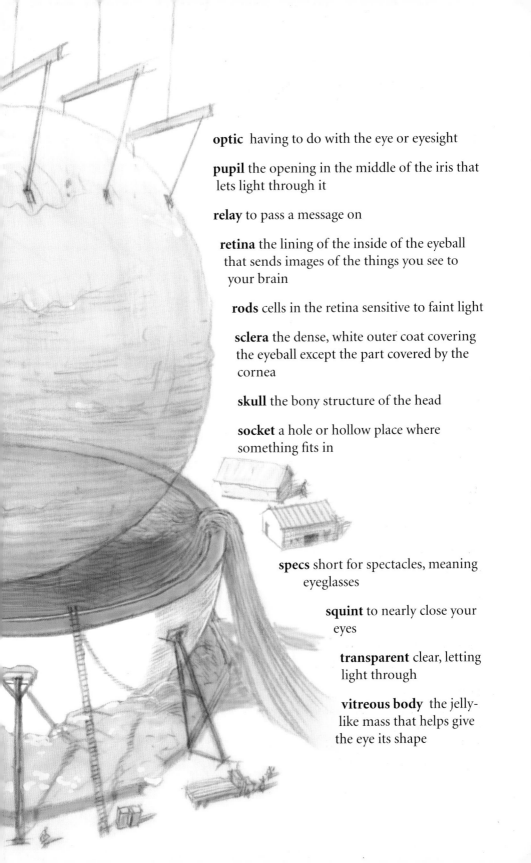

optic having to do with the eye or eyesight

pupil the opening in the middle of the iris that lets light through it

relay to pass a message on

retina the lining of the inside of the eyeball that sends images of the things you see to your brain

rods cells in the retina sensitive to faint light

sclera the dense, white outer coat covering the eyeball except the part covered by the cornea

skull the bony structure of the head

socket a hole or hollow place where something fits in

specs short for spectacles, meaning eyeglasses

squint to nearly close your eyes

transparent clear, letting light through

vitreous body the jelly-like mass that helps give the eye its shape

To Learn More

Animal Eyes by Beth Fielding. EarlyLight Books, 2011.

Crust & Spray: Gross Stuff in Your Eyes, Ears, Nose, and Throat by C. S. Larsen, illustrated by Michael Slack. Millbrook Press, 2009.

Eyes and Ears by Seymour Simon. HarperCollins, 2005.

My Travelin' Eye by Jenny Sue Kostecki-Shaw. Henry Holt and Co., 2008.

All About the Senses (DVD), produced and directed by Fabian-Baber. Schlessinger Media, 2006.

The National Eye Institute/National Institutes of Health: See All You Can See

isee.nei.nih.gov/parts/visualsystem.asp

KidsHealth®: Your Eyes

kidshealth.org/kid/htbw/eyes.html

Thanks to: Kate Waters, Lois Smith, and Susan Bloom

Index